With the Eye of Faith

Meditations and Prayers

With the Eye of Faith
Meditations and Prayers

Patrick Sookhdeo

Isaac Publishing

With the Eye of Faith: Meditations and Prayers

First edition, 2020

Published in the United States of America by Isaac Publishing
1934 Old Gallows Road, Suite 350
Vienna VA 22182

Library of Congress Control Number: 2020946089
ISBN: 978-1-952450-04-4
Printed in the United Kingdom

Contents

From the author

This is a book of meditations and prayers that have uplifted, encouraged or comforted me at various times of my life. I hope they will be a blessing to others too.

Please do not look on them as poetic works to be judged on their literary merit. I am not a poet. But I have sought to explore and embrace a variety of styles of communication, some of them from the east, where my roots are.

The reader will notice fragments of hymns or other writings that have touched me. I would love to thank each author who has unwittingly contributed in this way, but I think they are all in heaven.

What I can do is express my deep gratitude to the colleagues who have helped me arrange the meditations and prayers in order and have designed the book so beautifully. And above all I want to thank my beloved Saviour, who found me, called me, leads me – and pours out on me His daily grace, not least through some of the words included in these pages.

Patrick Sookhdeo
Pewsey, September 2020

Introduction

What is the purpose of human existence?

God has created us in His own Divine image and although sin and rebellion have marred the image there still exists within us that fundamental desire for our Creator. This is the tragedy of the human race. We turned against Him who made us. We rebelled against the command of the One who gave us our very existence. We rejected the Source of all life in order to eat forbidden fruit, only to find it brought no satisfaction. We are left with a longing that will be satisfied with nothing but God Himself, a thirst that cannot be quenched except by immersing ourselves in Him.

Human beings' primary desire is for happiness and fulfilment, but these can only truly be found in a relationship with Him who made us in His image. Augustine, writing from North Africa in the late fourth century, was right in affirming that God has made us for Himself and our hearts are restless until they find their rest in Him. It can be stated further that our hearts will find no happiness until that broken relationship is restored and we live as it were in our primordial state in Eden. There our first parents existed in an unbroken relationship with their Maker. There they enjoyed an intimate communion with Him. There they experienced perfect bliss and a satisfaction that desired nothing else. What is it we seek but to return to Eden, which was closed to us when they embraced wrong desires and so created the emptiness and longing which all subsequent generations have experienced – the longing that nothing but God can satisfy, the emptiness which nothing but He can fill?

What is salvation but a return to Eden, a restoration of broken relationship, a renewal of the Divine image? The seed of the woman shall crush the serpent's head – and so He did, on the cross. For in His death He defeated Satan, sin and death and thereby lifted death's curse. Adam's seed can now rise with Him to victory. Eden is again open to us. Intimacy with our Creator God is re-established. We can begin to experience the blissful blessedness of which Jesus spoke in the Beatitudes.

And yet the insatiable longing continues throughout our earthly lives, even after we have turned to God in repentance. For the more we have of Him, the more we want of Him.

More than twelve centuries after Augustine, on another continent, English and Scottish theologians and parliamentarians formulated a catechism for children that asserted: "Man's chief end is to glorify God, and to enjoy him forever."[1]

So the God we love is not only our rest and peace but also our joy and delight.

Made in the image of God, *imago dei*, we have souls and consciences. We humans, alone in all creation, have been made with the capacity to know God and have a relationship with Him. It is only we who have restless hearts longing to find their rest in Him. While all creation can bring Him glory, only humans can enjoy God.

We are not only made **by** God, we are made **for** God. We are incomplete without Him. Hence our longing for our Beloved, a longing to fill ourselves with Him, delight ourselves in Him, refresh ourselves in Him, and rest our restless hearts in Him.

To spend time in His presence is the essence of meditative prayer. The more we do so, the more we find the peace and joy we are made for. As a cow slowly chews the cud, gradually extracting nutrition and goodness from the grass she grazed, so we "chew" again and again on God's Word, on His Divine *Logos* who is His eternal Son, letting His Spirit feed our souls, as more and more depths are revealed to us. This meditation leads us to the contemplation and adoration of our Beloved, the Lord Jesus Christ, in Whom we find the ultimate bliss that satisfies all our desires. And the more we contemplate Him in silent love, the more we reflect Him.

The apostle Paul describes how the desire to know Christ was his driving motivation and passion:

> I consider everything a loss because of the surpassing worth of knowing Christ Jesus my Lord ... I want to know Christ (Philippians 3:8,10)

We can find similar blessing by "chewing" on the words of other believers – their hymns and songs, their prayers and other writings. Human experience is richly diverse. Various Church traditions have opened to believers many ways of stilling their restless hearts and kindling their spiritual joy. Christians of different cultures naturally have different starting points in their encounter with God. As we grow in our Christian lives, and mature in our discipleship, we may find blessing in new ways of drawing close to the Lord, ways that lacked impact for us in the past. We may find fresh inspiration by borrowing from fellow believers from other places or times the words, music, art, or spiritual disciplines that are the norm for them.

God can speak to us in the most surprising "texts". The sailor and adventurer Sir Francis Drake wrote on 17 May 1587 to Sir Francis

Walsingham, the "spy-master" of England's Queen Elizabeth I, "There must be a begynnyng of any great matter, but the contenewing unto the end untyll it be thoroughly ffynyshed yeldes the trew glory."[2] Drake was thinking of military matters when he wrote to Walsingham, but his words were later developed into an inspirational prayer:

> Lord God, when thou givest to thy servants to endeavour any great matter, grant us also to know that it is not the beginning, but the continuing of the same, until it be thoroughly finished, that yieldeth the true glory; through him who, for the finishing of thy work, laid down his life for us, our Redeemer, Jesus Christ. Amen.[3]

This prayer was used for Britain's second National Day of Prayer during the Second World War, and since then on many other occasions. It is very applicable to the whole Christian life, to any venture for God, and to the search – by prayer and meditation – for that place of rest and joy in His heart.

Likewise God can teach us through surprising objects – a red thread, a vast ocean, a human hand. He can remind us of "the old, old story" or He can reveal to us fresh depths of His truth. And what He teaches us, as we take time to listen to Him in meditative prayer, is often surprising too. The Beatitudes tell us that a blessed happiness can come, amongst other sources, from poverty of spirit, mourning, and being persecuted and falsely accused. Such deep spiritual truths are like the cow's grass – they can only be absorbed, digested and appropriated by chewing them over in the Lord's presence through long meditation and prayer.

The blessing described in the Beatitudes is gained during our time as believers on earth, which is an in-between time. We have left Egypt, the land of oppression and bondage, and crossed the Red Sea, our conversion and baptism, but we have not yet entered the Promised Land, heaven. We are in the wilderness, a place of wandering, a dangerous place fraught with conflict, with gruelling hardships and suffering, and with many doubts and temptations. The soul journeying through this life will experience not only sin and failure but also faith and joy, not only periods of deep darkness but mountain-top experiences. John Bunyan wrote brilliantly of this in his 1678 book *Pilgrim's Progress*. But if we view the negative experiences with the eye of faith, we make them positives. We discover, like Bunyan's Christian, that the lions are chained. We realise, like Bunyan's Mr Valiant-for-Truth, that our scars are badges of honour, a precious witness to the spiritual battles we have fought in the wilderness, through which our faith has been strengthened and purified. We come to understand that the struggles of our wilderness journey are a blessing that enable us to grow in the knowledge of God and to still our restless hearts; thus they can, indeed, bring us the bliss of the Beatitudes.

The ninety-eight meditations and prayers in this book are intended to take us into the realm of the spirit, where we encounter God and His love in a variety of situations, whether abject despair, imminent death, loneliness, alienation, rejection or other suffering, or intense and thrilling joy or overwhelming peace.

May God bless us all as we follow in the steps of our Lord Jesus, journeying together to our heavenly Home, learning from one another and from His Spirit, and may he satisfy our longings with that vision of Himself.

1 Westminster Assembly, *The Westminster Shorter Catechism. With Scripture Proofs*, Edinburgh: Banner of Truth Trust, 1977.
2 John Barrow, *The Life, Voyages, and Exploits of Admiral Sir Francis Drake, Knt*, London, United Kingdom: John Murray, 1843, pp. 233-234.
3 Eric Miner-White, *Daily Prayer*, London: Oxford University Press, 1941.

In His image

*"So God created mankind in his own image,
in the image of God he created them;
male and female he created them."*

—Genesis 1:27

Reflection

The Spirit of God shall look out
Through the believer's gaze,
And the believer shall reveal
The Saviour's face,
Reflecting the visage
Of their Beloved.

All creation, laud Him King

All creation, laud Him King,
Lord of the universe, space and time
Ruler of the heavenly sphere
Supreme Master is He.

All of life before Him bow
The angelic hosts praise Him now
The elders round the Throne magnify Him
Whom the saints in heaven and earth adore.

He is the centre and sun.
Light of my light, ever burning bright,
Light of light and life of life
Guiding me through the darkest night.

And will you not then, my soul,
Your sovereign Master adore?
Will you not own Him Lord
Till mortality has ceased and eternity is embraced?

O Divine Intelligence

O Divine Intelligence,
Triune God, Creator and Sustainer,
Whose omniscience spans all time,
Whose knowledge knows no end.
Reason and Truth were revealed
When the Divine Logos came down.
He who was eternal, before life's dawn,
Ineffably appeared in time.
Spirit of God, reveal Your will
And guide my hand to choose the right,
The excellent, the pleasing to You.

By Your reason, my mind can start to see
A glimpse of Him who spanned eternity
Yet took His place amongst humanity
And at Calvary was crucified for me.
Now Your sacred mysteries are before me,
Which, by Your grace, I appropriate,
So that they become food and drink for me.
As Your flesh and blood I take
Your life in mine does flow
And sweet Your presence to me becomes
As the Divine Logos in me dwells.

Now I am no longer my own.
To Him I belong.
He, Reason, became my reason to be
So that His Divine Will might be fulfilled,
And even in this frail body of mine
The Divine Illumination be displayed
To the glory of His eternal Son.
Light of my life and Life of my life,
Take my will and make it Your own.
For in relinquishing my will, I am set free
And own that my will now belongs to You.

Ocean drops

Mere drops in the ocean are we,
Insignificant,
Just molecules sliding.
Yet what is the ocean
But a multitude of drops
Which, when brought together,
Display such terrifying form?
Yes, ocean drops are we,
Each possessed with infinite value,
Created by the Divine.

His incarnation

"The Word became flesh and made his dwelling among us. We have seen his glory, the glory of the one and only Son, who came from the Father, full of grace and truth."

—John 1:14

The Divine incarnate

He the Lord of heaven and earth
Sovereign majestic King of the universe
Ruler and Sustainer of all life
Descends to earth and becomes man.

Taking human flesh, He enters our humanity
Divesting Himself of all riches and honour
He becomes a servant –
The Lord of Glory is a slave.

Divine incarnate, in poverty He dies
With naught but the clothes He wore
Devoid of all things, destitute He lived,
Dependent, yet serving with never ending compassion
The weak, the infirm, the vulnerable, the rejected.
Whilst poor He made others rich
Out of His bountiful mercy and grace
He brought love where there was hate
Peace where there was discord
Goodness where there was selfishness
Generosity where there was greed.

Yet despised and rejected was He.
Disavowed by the very subjects He served
Falsely accused and to the authorities handed over
Found guilty and condemned,
A criminal sentenced to ignominious death
On the tree of shame
Tortured, brutalised, nailed on the cross of pain.

"My God, my God, why have You forsaken Me?" He cries
And in darkness He dies
To the grave He descends
Forsaken and alone
Yet to rise triumphant
With new life abundant He lives
And pours out this life to all.

Incarnate again, He comes
To His brothers and sisters poor
And destitute of all life's goods,
He shows in abundance His love
To the despised and rejected
He welcomes with warm embrace
And bestows honour and worth.
On their sick, suffering and hungry.
He showers upon them His care and compassion.
Accepted in the Beloved, they became His own
But the haughty who bear His Name
He will despise
The rich He will send away empty
The powerful He will put down and humble
Then He the King will reign
In terror and judgement
On those who call His Name
And own Him as Lord
Yet despise and reject His way
In pretence they lie
But retribution is near
For justice and mercy will reign
Over those are who truly His own
And bear His Name.

Alethea

Truth roams as a beggar
Clothed in simple attire,
Seeking a home it goes door to door,
Rejected and unwanted.

Lies, though, finds open doors.
For dressed in resplendent robes
And jewelled turban,
It has no need to seek a home
But is readily embraced.

Yet Truth yearns to be welcomed.
For with Truth would come freedom,
Liberty that sets the captives free.

Freed from the tinsel and glamour
Seen in its truest form
Alethea, reality, the only Truth,
Bringing freedom from guilt and sin,
The only true liberty setting the captive free

For Truth is Jesus
Alethea
Reality
The only true.

Jesus, salvation's horn

Jesus, salvation's horn
In a humble stable born
Freedom from Satan's tyranny, He will bring
And destruction of death's deadly sting.
With ox and ass and cross-shadowed brow He lay
Asleep in the cradle made of hay.
Though Sovereign God and Master He
Servant and slave chose to be,
Rejected and despised
With visage marred
Crown of thorns He wore
And on that cruel cross He bore
Our sins that we may sin no more
And so we love that love that becamest poor.
Frankincense, myrrh and gold we now bring
And with all in heaven and earth to the Christ Child we sing
Glory, honour and praise belong alone to Him.

Made man

Great is Thy goodness,
O matchless Lord.

Come, let us sing
Of Him who died
The sinner's death
That we might
Live and holy be.
Come, let us sing
Of Him who came
Incarnate was He,
God incomprehensible
Made man.
Come, let us sing
Of He who alone is worthy
Of our love and adoration,
God incomparable
Made man.

Sweetest Saviour
Dearest Master
How precious Thou art to me.
Thy love spans the heavens,
Thy mercy reaches the depths of the sea,
Thy faithfulness flows
Unceasing like rivers,
Thy grace is unending, whose
Never-ending supply
Can never be exhausted.

Crowned are You,
Lord and King.
All heaven and earth
Sea and sky,
All creation owns You Lord
And kneels at Your feet.

Children

At Ramah the mothers' grief is heard
As children are put to the sword.
For baby Jesus they seek
To end His earthly life
That He will be no more Lord and King.
And so throughout the ages
The children suffer
For with their end
Christ is no more
And faith dies.

Iridescent light

Shine, iridescent Light
Burn with radiance bright
Illuminating the darkness
O the Christ Child, Man King, Saviour God,
With resplendence descend
And lighten our way.

O Christ Child,
Shine with iridescent light.
O Man King,
Burn with radiance bright
O Saviour God,
With resplendence descend

With glory our faces shine
When Jesus we meet
At the mercy seat
And the all-consuming fire
Melts the coldness of our hearts,
Setting our souls aglow.

Nothing but the blood

"For you know that it was not with perishable things such as silver or gold that you were redeemed from the empty way of life handed down to you from your ancestors, but with the precious blood of Christ, a lamb without blemish or defect."

—1 Peter 1:18-19

Shame

Forsaken by God, betrayed by man,
There on the cross, alone in agony,
Despised, rejected, a creature of shame,
Ignominious You die,
Nailed to an accursed tree.

Divine community

Divine humanity
Created in the Divine image
Reflecting His glory,
Possessed with dignity
Endowed with worth
Shared blood in their veins doth flow
A family one are they.

Divine community
Created by Divine sacrifice
A people bought with Jesus' shed blood
And in their veins that blood doth flow,
Covenant love binds together,
One Spirit possesses all,
A loving unity.

Now nation, race and tribe
Are vanished and gone,
For all are one in Him.
His blood-bought people are they,
To love one another is their call
Each other's suffering to embrace
To care for one and all.

Good Friday Meditation I

Since the time Adam left
Humankind has been bereft
For Paradise was no more,
Its entrance closed for evermore.
Sin had taken its dreadful toll,
Suffering and death mankind bore.

Angelic hosts blocked the way
With flaming sword to keep at bay
All those who had gone astray.
God's anger against our race
Brought us all into shame and disgrace
With dreadful Judgement to face.

But now the gate is open once more,
Entrance to eternity restored,
For the cross the man Christ has mounted
And there suffering and death were defeated
By the shedding of His life-blood
All mankind was reconciled to God.

Feasting on the heavenly food

Come, celebrate this glorious festival,
Feast on the heavenly food
In remembrance of Him who died,
Of Him who gave His life to set us free
With body broken and blood shed
He died for me on that cruel tree.
Now He calls us to remember Him
For He who was dead now lives again
And with all the glorious host of heaven
And the worldwide communion of saints
We rejoice and partake of His feast,
We eat of the heavenly bread
And drink of the life-giving wine.
We partake of the broken flesh
And of the shed blood
And so we feast
His flesh becomes our flesh
His blood is our blood,
Flesh for flesh, blood for blood,
He dwells in us
And we in Him.

Good Friday Meditation II

Love, endless love,
Knowing no limits
Having no end
Eternal is its nature
Yet incarnate
Love of all loves the best
Love, such love, incarnate
In my heart now dwells.

Love, endless love,
Knowing no limits
Having no end
Love, such love,
Such wondrous love,
Incarnate – all other loves excelling –
In my heart does dwell
In abandonment.
I give myself to that love
To be possessed
With love Divine
And know endless love,
Jesus, as heaven fills my heart.

I will love You,
O my Lord,
Till the end of time
And eternity begins.

Endless is Your love,
O my Lord, to me
A love that loves,
To the completion of love itself.

Now my love,
O my Lord,
Is but a reflection of Your love,
Love that only gives.

Love incarnate came down,
O my Lord,
And revealed the selflessness of love
That gave of itself on the cross.

I carry the nailprints of Your love
Embedded on the palms of my hands,
Imprinted on my heart.
Your love fills my soul.

Love, endless love,
Knowing no limits
Having no end,
Eternity is its nature.
Love, endless love
Love without limits
Love without end
Love, such love,
Love, such wondrous love,
Love of all other loves the best
Incarnate in my heart does dwell.
In abandonment

I give myself to that love
To be possessed
With love Divine.

Love betrayed,
Love yet loves:
Love loves in selfishness
Love loves in denial
Love loves in cowardice
Love loves in pride and conceit
Love gives
Love sacrifices
Love dies.

Love lives.
Love dies.
Love lives again.
For love eternal can never die.
Embraced in everlasting arms,
Love triumphs,
Love conquers death.
What love is this
Which has vanquished death,
Which lives in the Victor's breast,
Never to be separated?
For love and Victor are the same
And love lives for evermore.

On the tree of shame

Goodness where there was selfishness,
Generosity where there was greed,
Yet despised and rejected was He,
Disowned by the very subjects He saved,
Handed over to the authority,
Falsely accused and He was tried,
Guilty was found and condemned,
A criminal was He
Sentenced to ignominious death
On the tree of shame,
Tortured, brutalised and nailed
On the cross of shame.
Rejected by man, rejected by God,
"My God, my God, why have you forsaken me?" He cries.
And in the darkness He dies.
To the grave He descends,
Forsaken and alone,
And yet to rise triumphant,
With new life abundant.
He lives and continues to give our life to all.

O weave the threads of the eternal covenant

O weave the threads
That make the cords
That bind us to Himself.
He makes us captives, bound
So that we cannot escape.
The cords are scarlet that speak
Of the covenant born of sacrifice.
It is an eternal bond,
Its cord stained by His blood,
Shed for me, a sinner,
Bound, yet loved,
By an eternal pledge
That can never be broken.

His victory

"Death has been swallowed up in victory."

—1 Corinthians 15:54

He reigns

Christ in majesty reigns.

Over time and space
He reigns.
Over the universe of worlds
He reigns.
Over all creation
He reigns.
Over the rulers of the earth
He reigns.

Christ reigns.

Over His Church
Does He reign?
Over me
Does He reign?

Reign in me, precious Lord,
Reign in me.

The Lord has conquered

The Lord has conquered.
Victorious is He,
Magnificently He reigns.
Heaven and earth ring with His glory.
Satan is defeated,
His evil hosts vanquished.
Death has lost its sting,
The grave its victory.
So, Christian, follow Him,
Join in His triumphal train.

Cover the way with flowers

Cover the way with flowers,
Clap your hands – rejoice.
For Jesus the Way is glorified,
For Jesus the Way is adored.
Dance together, sing alleluia,
For Heaven's Way is worshipped,
For into heaven we enter,
With Christ adored, our Way.

Cover the way with flowers,
Clap your hands – rejoice.
For Jesus the Way is glorified.
Dance together, sing alleluia,
For Satan the enemy is defeated
And into heaven we enter,
Covered with Jesus' sprinkled precious blood
To meet with Christ our Way.

Fear

"So do not fear, for I am with you;
do not be dismayed, for I am your God.
I will strengthen you and help you;
I will uphold you with my righteous right hand."

—Isaiah 41:10

When fears arise

When fears arise
And storm clouds fill the skies,
When darkness deepens,
And sight grows dim,
And turns to endless night,
Be Thou my guide.

Lighten the darkness,
Dispel the gloom,
And in Thy presence let me hide.
Turn Thou my night to day,
Chase my fears far away
And let me there abide.

Face thou thy fear

Face thou thy fear
For the Saviour, He is near.

Make firm your stand
And He will grasp your hand.

Cast doubt aside
And let Him decide.

Lean on His heavenly breast,
His purposes are best.

Question not His gentle care
But see His loving tear.

Yes, see His tear-filled searching eye
For it's on you His gaze doth lie.

We do not fear

We do not fear
Because the Saviour is near,

He Who such pain did bear
For those He counts most dear.

On the cross He lay
For all my debts to pay.

Such suffering He endured
When my sins He bore.

Now in His footsteps I tread.
And no curse will I dread.

Like Him I am broken bread
And with Him my blood is shed.

The Shepherd is gone

The streams run dry
The grass withers
The Shepherd is gone
His rod and staff no more.
The wolf prowls
And the lion roars,
Serpents abound.

In the heat of the day
And the cold of the night
My soul lies parched
With nothing to refresh,
No one to guide or protect.
My soul knows no rest.

Pursued I am,
Not by the hound of heaven
But by an enemy who knows no remorse
Dark is the valley
And fearsome the night.

The feast is over.
The meat is gone.
The bread and wine no more.
For sustenance I yearn
For rest I plead,
For God my Shepherd
Again to lead me
Beside the waters of balm
To feed me on the soft pasture,
To know protection and care
And in His presence abide.

Speak, Lord

Speak, O Lord, speak
That I may hear
Your still small voice
Crystal clear

Not in the earthquake
Nor through the terror of the storm
But with your still small voice,
Speak, Lord, still.

Speak words of comfort
Words of tenderness
Words of soothing balm
Words to bring healing calm

Speak, Lord, that I may hear
"Fear not for I am with you.
And I will be with you,
With you for evermore."

I have heard Your voice, Lord,
Calling me to serve You,
Yes, I will be Your servant
Here I am, Lord, send me

And in Your will I shall delight,
In Your strength I shall rest,
In Your Word I shall trust,
For Your words are life.

Pain

"Then I would still have this consolation – my joy in unrelenting pain – that I had not denied the words of the Holy One."

—Job 6:10

Job and unending pain

What pain that falls
Drop upon drop on the troubled heart,
In the brightness of the day,
In the darkness of the night.
There is no respite
From the endless pain that flows
Ceaselessly across the vicissitudes of life.

Must it always be, this endless pain?
Yes, for humanity is brought forth in pain,.
Yes, for the course of earthly existence.
The vision of a painless life
Is but an illusion that cannot be fulfilled.
Except when, as a gift, it's given.
The prayer to be set free from pain
Should be instead "They will be done."

Rather, pain must be embraced
And God's majestic grace allowed to work,
He our sufficiency in all realms of being.
It is thus the soft dew drops of calm descend
Upon the anguished soul
And joy finds its way through the maze of pain
Bringing a heavenly peace
Into the depths of woe.

And there is Another who knows endless pain.
Across eternity's span.
My kinsman-Redeemer, who bore my pain
In a heart that would be broken
By the pain of love rejected.
And I have this consolation,
My joy in unrelenting pain,
That I have not denied the words of Him
Who gave Himself for me.

Pain

Worthlessness
Vanity
Emptiness
Stupidity
Failure

The pain that teaches
The pain that strengthens
The pain that purifies
The pain of empathy
The Pain of Sacrifice.

Why are You silent, O my Lord?

Why are You silent, O my Lord?
Why do You not hear my cry
And feel my anguish and pain?
For night is far spent
Yet there is no dawn.
Darkness has consumed the light.
When, O Dayspring, will You come?
When, O bright Morning Star, will You appear?
When will hope, like the almond bud, blossom
In the desolation and barrenness of life?

Walk with me, Jesus

Walk with me, Jesus,
For dark is the night
And hard the road.
Jesus, walk with me.

Walk with me, Jesus,
For great is my suffering
And endless my sorrows.
Jesus, walk with me.

Walk with me, Jesus,
For many are my trials
And with no respite.
Jesus, walk with me.

Walk with me, Jesus,
For I am alone
With none beside me.
Jesus, walk with me.

Walk with me, Jesus,
For You are my Friend.
Hold my hand, Jesus,
Till my journey's end.

With the eye of faith

*"Now faith is confidence in what we hope for and
assurance about what we do not see."*

—Hebrews 11:1

Penetrating the darkness

Penetrating the darkness, God is seen
With eye of faith. The clouds of doubt
And fear that hid His face
Are dispelled.

Now through the darkness, God is seen
With eye of faith, at last, at last,
No doubts or fears to block my sight,
Behold my Saviour, precious, dear.

So glory descends
With holy fire.

Moses – so veil must be worn

God was in the cloud,
The dense, dark, smoking, thunderous cloud,
Lightning and loud trumpet blast.
The people trembled,
The mountain quaked,
Moses spoke
And God answered.

In the darkness, God is heard.

So veil must be worn
To conceal what has been borne
Standing in the Divine presence,
Face aglow with radiance.

So veil must be worn
To conceal the Divine splendour
Shining in fullest glory
From man reflecting deity.

On the sea of life

Lord, keep me safe on the sea of life,
The winds blow, the storms rage,
The waves crash,
My boat is overwhelmed.

But You, Lord, are there.
Your presence is with me,
Though asleep yet awake,
For nothing is hid from You.

When all seemed lost
With a word the storms stills,
The waves subside
And all is calm

Why did you doubt,
O my unbelieving soul?
Why were you afraid,
Why did your faith fail?

Lord, I looked and saw the storms
And fear filled my heart.
Why did You not act
To save Your erring child?

My Saviour dear
Though asleep was ever watchful
And with omniscient eye
He saw and cared.

And with omnipotent rebuke
Controlled all nature's forces,
With simple words commanded:
Quiet! Be still!

I see You not but with the eye of faith

Hungry was I
In want of food
  When, O Lord, did I feed you?
When you fed my brothers and sisters.

Hungry was I, in desperate want
Food you did provide, my hunger you satisfied
  But when, O my Lord, did I feed you,
  For I see You not but with the eye of faith?
When you fed the least of My brothers and sisters
Then you were feeding me.

  Who are these my lowly brethren - are they the sons and
    daughters of Adam's race?
  Or are they children of the new covenant, of the new
    creation, of a heavenly Kingdom,
  Born of the Spirit, bone of my bone, flesh of my flesh,
    blood of my blood?

On that Judgement Day
The least and lowliest of My children
Shall feast on My heavenly manna
Shall drink from My rivers of life
Shall be healed by the leaves of My trees
Shall be clothed with celestial robes
Shall be set free from all sin and suffering
Shall be embraced in My eternal arms.

Matthew 25:31-46

I will not deny You

Though the winds of adversity roar
And the storms of calamity rage
I will not deny You.
Though the waves crash
And turmoil reigns
I will not deny You.
Though fears overwhelm
And faith recedes
I will not deny You.

Deny you, my Lord, I never shall.
I bear the cross on the palms of my hands
That I will not deny You.
I bear the cross on my forehead
That I will not deny You.

For you have made me Your own.
You will not deny me.
For you have engraved me
On the palms of your hands.
You will not deny me.
For Your Name is written
On my forehead.
I will not deny You.

For your eyes are ever upon me.
You will not deny me.
For your heart is filled with tenderness.
You will not deny me.
For your presence is ever with me.
You will not deny me.

For you are my Master and Friend.
I am your adopted blood-bought child.
You will not deny me.

Isaiah 49:16; Revelation 22:4

How can I betray You, O Lord?

How can I betray You, O Lord,
Who gave Your all for me
With thorn-crowned brow
And nail-pierced hands and feet,
With blood and water flowing
From Your wounded side?
You look down on me
With eyes awash with tears
Of love and infinite pity.
Kneeling beneath Your feet, O Lord,
I look up and meet
Those tender eyes,
Drawing me to You
And so I worship and adore
And crown You Lord of all.

Repentance and forgiveness

"If we claim to be without sin, we deceive ourselves and the truth is not in us. If we confess our sins, he is faithful and just and will forgive us our sins and purify us from all unrighteousness."

—*1 John 1:8-9*

Repentance

My God, my Way, my Truth,
My all, my Redeemer, my Saviour, my defender
My friend, my very life itself.
In Thee is my all in all.
All that I will ever want or need.
Thou art my fulfiller.
Thou suppliest my every need,
O Lord, but what I need most
Is all of Thee.
Thy strength, thy love, thy wisdom,
Thy touch.

Now as my manifold sins are before me,
My failures before mine eyes,
I need Thee more than ever.

Slowly my strength decreases
My energy saps out of me.
O my failures, my sins,
Why have you overcome me?
Why am I defeated?
Do I not know my Lord?
Will He not forgive
Will He not return,
Will He not strengthen me
Will He not place
My feet on solid rock?

O Lord, my all in all,
Come to me again
And pour out Thy Spirit of life
And hope upon me.
O uplift me, my Father,
Let me feel Thee.
O how I need Thee,
I need Thee,
Every passing second
I need Thee more.
How can I live without Thee?
O my Lord,
Subdue this vileness within me
With Thy love and grace
Cast out the evil.
Cleanse me, wash me,
Purify me,
Uplift my heart to Thee.

Lord, I have nothing to offer Thee
But my life, which is worthless,
My soul, which is filthy,
My love, which is feeble,
My faith, which is weak.

Lord, if Thou canst use it
Then use it for Thy glory,
I know that I have caused Thee grief,
Pain and tears
But, Lord ,teach me Thy way
That I may be
Thy faithful servant

Broken cisterns

What is there to gain
When it brings so much pain?
That which we pursue
But cannot subdue?

What is it of life's pleasure
That can be experienced without measure
Yet only leaves the soul empty
And with doubts and fears a-plenty?

I am yearning, parched and dry,
I go to draw water to satisfy,
But the water I crave has run away,
I must try again another day.

Again I return, again despair,
The cistern is empty and needs repair,
The waters that would my thirst slake
Drained away as the vessel did break

And so the eye cries
As life slowly dies
For all that was sought
With money could not be bought.

To accept the gift that He gave
Is what the soul craves
To know that heavenly bliss
And live in the eternal caress.

The liar

The liar's pathway is destruction.
With his siblings, falsehood and deception,
They walk the broad highway to perdition
As they follow their father the devil's instructions.
Their malice knows no bounds,
They pursue like panting hounds
With treachery in their pounding hearts
Until their victim is torn apart.

As they strike with sharpened claws,
Set on vengeance without cause,
All good things they misconstrue
Making ugly what is true.
One end, one goal, one thing they seek -
That their hate might be complete
For forgiveness has no place
In hearts impossible to placate.

So, Christian, consider now and repent,
That your Father in heaven may relent.
You are treading a road to the father of lies.
He who travels that road is he who dies,
For hellfire awaits
From which there is no escape.
The gnawing conscience will never be assuaged
And it will be too late, too late, too late.

Assurance of freedom from guilt's tyranny

Divine assurance You have given
To me a sinner now forgiven.
To you, my crucified Lord, I cried
For on that cross You bled and died
And all my sins away You took
And promised never more to look
On them, so with glad heart I rise.
My eager hand will grasp the prize
Of freedom from guilt's tyranny,
Forever Yours with certainty.

Praying hands

"As long as Moses held up his hands..."

—Exodus 17:11

Pray for me, carry me, rescue me

Jesus, God's right hand,
Pray for me.
Jesus, Son of the Father,
Pray for me.
Jesus, Divine Intercessor
Pray for me.

In Your mighty power,
Carry me.
In Your beloved arms,
Carry me.
Close to Your heart,
Carry me.

From all evil intent,
Rescue me.
From the terrors of the night,
Deliver me.
From want and despair,
Provide for me.

For You sit at the right hand of God
To plead my cause,
For You conquered sin and death
For my gain, my redemption,
And rose triumphant from the grave
To be my sovereign Lord.

How can I not then trust You,
My dear loving Saviour,
Who ever watches over me
By day and by night,
Whose everlasting arms
Enfold me?

For I am never far from You,
I am always in Your sight.
No ill can befall me
Outside of Your Divine will
With You ever near.
Under Your Divine protection I live
With You as my light and guide
And so I will trust in You,
My Divine Intercessor and Friend.

Praying hands

The hand, unity and form, wholeness,
The fingers, diversity in unity,

The thumb,
Removed but essential,
Vital if hand is to grip.
The Thumb is God – essential to life
Essential for His people,
God our Father, we worship and adore.

The forefinger,
Closest to me –
Our nearest and dearest,
Our friends and family,
And God's family too,
His sons and daughters – our brothers and sisters
His family, our family.
For them we pray – in their need,
In their distress, in their grief and pain we pray,
In their joy and pleasure we rejoice.

The middle finger,
The tallest, the strongest –
Give prayer for those in authority,
Our church leaders, our governments, those who rule over us,
Whose power is given from above,
Who need Solomon's wisdom and knowledge.
Pray for them, that we may live peaceful and quiet lives
In all godliness and holiness.

The fourth finger,
The weakest –
The sick in body or mind,
The needy, the lonely, the rejected,
The vulnerable, the victims, the persecuted,
Those who suffer for Christ,
Enduring hardships for their love and faith in Him.
God knows each one, as I pray for them all.

The little finger,
The smallest and lowliest – is me,
Nothing but a sparrow, sold for a halfpenny,
Who yet can approach the throne of grace,
Can pour out my heart, for He already knows,
Can kneel at His feet, in turmoil or peace,
With words and songs, with groans and tears,
And cast my cares on Him.

So my hand is a prayer.
I see the unity, oneness, diversity, plurality.
All life is a whole:
God, His people, His world, humanity.
See the story of the weak,
The highest and the lowliest,
Me a part of the whole,
Needing God – essential to live.
The hands, praying hands, that say much of prayer.

Holy Spirit, groan for me

Holy Spirit,
Groaning with unexpressed words,
Intercede for me.

When my pathway is hid,
Holy Spirit, pray for me.
When God's will is unknown,
Holy Spirit, intercede for me.

When I cannot find words,
Holy Spirit, pray for me.
When in deep distress,
Holy Spirit, intercede for me.

When tears overwhelm,
Holy Spirit, groan for me.

Romans 8:26

Tribulation and deliverance

"I have told you these things, so that in me you may have peace. In this world you will have trouble. But take heart! I have overcome the world."

—John 16:33

Forsaken

Lord, why were You forsaken,
    Abandoned
On that tree of curse and shame?
Why were You left
    Alone?

Lord, why did Your Father leave you
    Bereft
Of His presence and smile?
On that fateful day, He was
    Hidden.

Lord, why did He hide Himself,
    Uncaring,
While You bore my sins on the cross,
Despised by all the world and
    Rejected?

Lord, how does it feel – rejection,
    Betrayal
By Him who is Love itself?
What is it like when the Faithful One
    Turns His back?

Lord, in pain and agony,
   Anguish
Fills Your body and soul
Darkness descends,
   Despair
Cries out – My God, my God,
My God, my God, my God,
   Why?

Yet hope is near,
   Glory
Descends and darkness is banished,
Death's sting is no more.
   Resurrection
Trumpets victory over the grave.
Christ lives
   Evermore.

Truth, goodness and beauty

Where there is truth and goodness,
Beauty resides.
For truth sets us free
From life's falsehoods and snares,
And goodness
From life's degradation
And beauty like life's chrysalis
Is born anew.
For, in truth reality dawns,
Free from the tinsel and sham.
Jesus the Truth is revealed
And goodness follows in its train,
Virtue wrapped in loveliness,
Free from selfishness and pride.
Jesus the true good, the only God,
The all-beauteous One revealed.

Stillness and peace

Be still and know that I am God
For it is in stillness that You speak,
Your voice heard above the endless chatter
And meaningless noise and din.
My soul finds rest and repose
And there experiences transcendence and power,
Perfect peace and rest.

For it is in Your stillness,
Divine activity works
In quietude not in earthquake and storm
That Your mind is made known
And Your will is done,
Your presence realised
The stillness of Your creative power.

In Your Divine stillness I rest,
Laying my troubled head upon Your breast,
Relinquishing the worry, fret and care,
Enfolded in Your eternal arms,
I finally submit to Your loving embrace
And hear Your soothing voice say:
Peace, perfect peace, all is well.

God is in the darkness

Darkness, overwhelming darkness,
Darkness of deepest despair.
Evening has given way to night
The shadow of death dawns,
Not the dawn that ushers in the morn.
Fear descends, devoid of hope,
The terrors of the night reign.

Where is the dawn that ushers in the morn,
Radiant light, becoming bright,
Dispelling the gloom,
Banishing the darkness?
Hope arises as faith is renewed
For God is in the darkness
And He will abide with me.

Whether seen or unseen

Darkness, deepening darkness,
Fear, deepening fear,
Taking possession of the soul.
Shrouding with hopelessness
Wrapping in despair

God removed, absent,
Hidden by the clouds.
Light dispelled by blackest night,
Yet God remains,
Seen by the eye of faith.

For God is in the darkness,
His presence in the shadows,
Unseen, He is there,
His guiding hand
Leading in the night.

So, my soul,
Put your trust in God.
Whether seen or unseen,
His love will remain
And be ever the same.

His purposes are good
And in time the clouds will lift,
The darkness be dispelled,
And He in glorious light
Will turn night into day.

Fret not

Fret not nor care
For the Lord He is near.
He, sovereign, reigns over all,
His hand, strong to deliver,
And His arm to protect
Through His mighty power.

Great is His saving mighty power,
Eternal is His everlasting love.
Infinite grace abounds,
Matchless are His works.
Sufficient for every need
Is the Lord my shield and fortress.

My shield and my strong fortress He shall be,
When through the darkness I cannot see
And though fiery darts and snares abound
His promise He will keep
My every need to meet,
He'll never leave me nor forsake.

He never leaves, He's always near
His presence will sustain,
In every circumstance and trial.
Though mountains quake and winds roar
I cast my cares upon Him
And fret not.

That silken thread

Hope, the scarlet cord
That binds me to You.
Satan's fury cannot break
A silken thread
Soaked in crimson blood
Of Your undying covenant love.

Meditation on Psalm 40:1-3

Sing, O my soul,
The song of the soul set free,
For the Lord's strong hand lifted me up.

Sing to the Lord, O my soul,
For He has delivered me
From the trap set for me
From the pit of noises.

Sing of the deliverance He has wrought
From the pit of no escape.
He reached down with His mighty arm
And brought me up and set me on safe ground.
My salvation He brought.

Sing to the Lord, O my soul,
For He has directed my path.
He set my feet upon solid rock.
Safe and secure I stand.
And established His purposes for me.
With His hand He has led me.

Sing to the Lord, O my soul,
From a heart filled with devotion
For Him who loved me.
He has put a new song in my mouth,
A hymn of praise to my God
For me to sing my thanks
For His deliverance evermore.

Sing, O my soul,
The song of the soul set free
From the dreadful pit of noises
Where my cries for help
With deafening echoes tormented my soul.
From the pit of no escape,
With none to save,
With no hope of deliverance

So, my soul, sing
The song of the soul set free,
Sing of Him who loves me
With a love that would not let go
And came to me when no one else would
When destruction was certain
And rescued me
And made me to sing
The song of the soul set free.

Praise Him!

"Then I looked and heard the voice of many angels, numbering thousands upon thousands, and ten thousand times ten thousand. They encircled the throne and the living creatures and the elders. In a loud voice they were saying:
  'Worthy is the Lamb, who was slain,
    to receive power and wealth and wisdom and strength
    and honour and glory and praise!'"

—Revelation 5:11-12

I will sing my Redeemer's praise

I will sing my Redeemer's praise
The praise of Him who died for me.
Who suffered on the cruel cross
That I, a sinner, may be free.

For He gave His life for me
And saved my soul eternally
His heavenly peace He did bestow
That Divine assurance I could know.

Now no more the grave I fear
For it holds no victory
And death's sting is drawn
As I rise to eternity.

There I will sing my Redeemer's praise
With the angel host and saints above
I will gaze and worship and adore
And sing of the Worthy One evermore.

As a shepherd leads his flock

You lead Your people
As a shepherd leads his flock
Guarding, keeping, protecting, providing,
Laying down Your life for them,
Until they reach their heavenly pasture
Where they will suffer no more
For there is the Divine glory.
They will sing the song in praise of Him who died
And dwell in His presence
For evermore.

Blessings of the triune God

Blessing
Blessing
Blessing
The three-fold blessing
From the triune God
Three in one
One in three
The blessings of the Father
The blessings of the Son
The blessings of the Spirit
Three in one
One in three
Blessing abound
To the saints of God
Blessings overflowing
To all called by His Name
Blessings in times of need
Blessings in the hour of trial
Blessings in all of life's mortality
Blessings in all of life's uncertainty
Blessings in all of life's infirmity
Blessings in times of doubt and fear
Blessings in darkness and in death
Blessings Divine that lift to God,
From whom they come,

Blessings of love
Blessings of goodness
Blessings of grace
Blessings of joy
Blessing incarnate
Making holy
Consecrating all life
To the triune Divine
The source of all blessings

On the Face Divine

On the Face Divine
Glory doth shine, with iridescent light
Burning bright,
On he who has been given sight.

Now through the darkness
God is seen.
Penetrating clouds of doubt and fear.
God the infinite shines on man.

So veil must conceal
Divine radiance in man,
Now changed for ever,
Resplendent in light He gives.

On the Face Divine
Glory doth shine, reflecting on the seer
With light iridescent
Reflecting on the beholder present.

So veil must hide
What the witness has borne.
In man the Divine lives
And shines forth in glory.

With the eye of faith, God is seen,
God that ever has been,
Once hidden, now revealed,
Fear banished, faith triumphant.

Exodus 34:29-35

When shall I praise You?

When shall I praise You, my God and King?
When morn has come and day breaks
In the brightness of the noonday light.
When shadows have vanished
And night is no more?

Or will I praise You in the valley of the shadow,
And in the land of death
When darkness reigns supreme
And night is endless night,
When the eye of faith grows dim
And God's guiding hand cannot be seen
Nor His pathways discerned?

Yes, it is then that my soul
Shall rejoice in my God and King.
Why should my soul be dismayed?
Hope thou in God
Who is thy helper and stay.

Hail, King Jesus

Rose of Sharon
Beauty art Thou
Lily of the Valley
Altogether lovely

Bright Morning Star
Herald of dawn
Resplendent in glory
Radiant on high

Hail, King Jesus,
Earth praises
Angels worship
Heaven adores

How can I then not sing, feeble though I am,
Of Your infinite mercy and unfailing love?
In Your faithfulness I rejoice,
Which has kept me all the days of my life.

His persecuted Church

"If the world hates you, keep in mind that it hated me first. If you belonged to the world, it would love you as its own. As it is, you do not belong to the world, but I have chosen you out of the world. That is why the world hates you. Remember what I told you: 'A servant is not greater than his master.' If they persecuted me, they will persecute you also."

—John 15:18-20

Victim, Priest and King

Lord, why were You forsaken, abandoned
On that tree of curse and shame?
Why were you left alone,
Bereft of Your Father's love and care?

Today Your people seem forsaken,
Left alone in cruel hands,
Persecuted, violently abused, martyred.
Make real to them Your presence and Your love.

Lord, Victim, Priest and King,
Come to Your suffering people,
Heal their brokenness,
Bind up their wounds,
Remove their distress,
And be their hope and a future.

Lord, when will it come?

Lord, when will it come
When your people will be free?
Lord, when will it come
When there will be justice and equity?

Lord, when will You come
To set Your people free?
Lord, when will You come
To end their pain and misery?

Lord, come now to Your people,
Heal their wounds,
Calm their fears,
Free them from their enemies.

Lord, come now to Your people
And set them free.
Lord, come now, come
And give your people liberty.

Rivers of tears

Rivers of tears run from my eyes
Flowing endlessly
Like a never-ceasing stream
Eyes filled with grief
Overwhelmed by the suffering of my people
Knowing no respite
Until the God of heaven looks down and sees
Until Thou seest
O Lord of heaven, look down and see.

See, my eyes run rivers of tears
Flowing unceasingly
See, my eyes are like a never-ending stream
With rivers of tears my eyes do run
Flowing incessantly
Weeping for the sufferings of my people
For the oppression of the vulnerable
Eyes filled with grief
O Lord, see, hear and rescue.

Rivers of tears pour from my eyes
See, my eyes are like an ever-flowing stream
See, my eyes are filled with grief
At the destruction of my people
At the oppression of the powerless
At the defeat of the weak
They know no respite
Until Thou seest.
O Lord of heaven, look down and see.

O Divine Master

O Love, our defender,
Come now to be our protector
From all evil foes.

O Divine Master of Your people,
Whose grace is boundless
And mercy inexhaustible,
Enfold them in Your everlasting arms
And sustain them in their time of trial.

O Divine Protector of Your people,
Whose power is infinite
And sovereignty absolute,
Spread Your wings over Your suffering people
And protect them from all evil forces.

O Divine Comforter of Your people,
Whose love has no beginning
And compassion has no end,
Draw them into Your heavenly bosom
And give to them your heavenly rest.

Tears of the oppressed

Tears of the oppressed
Falling like rain
Coursing endlessly down,
Weeping that knows no relief,
But God in His heaven
Looks down and sees.

Tears of the oppressed
Falling like rain
Take up our cause.
Redeem our lives.
Save and deliver us.
Dry our eyes.

Lamentations 3:48

Why, O Lord, why?

Why, O Lord, why
Must Your people suffer
At the hands of evil men
Who set traps that they fall in,
Who devise ways for their destruction,
Who slander their name
And malign their character,
Who cause them injuries,
Hurts and pain,
Who pursue and hound,
Seeking their destruction?

Why, O Lord, why?
They are hurting.
They are crying.
They are shamed.
They are abused.
They die alone.

Why, O Lord, why
Does evil triumph
While good is reviled,
The unrighteous trumpet
While the godly are dismayed,
The persecutors rejoice
While the persecuted are abased?

Why, O Lord, why?
Will it never end?
In despair they hold up their hands,
Crying to highest heaven
For You to hear
For You to see
For you to act
For you to come and deliver.
Why, O Lord, why?

They forsake You not.
Faithful are they
Who in deepest agony
Abhor You not,
Who, reviled and abused,
Reject You not.
Who, faced with the cross,
Despise You not.

Why, O Lord, why?
O that they may know
Your tender care,
That binds them to You,
Enfolded in Your arms,
Your steadfast love
That never ends
Your strength that will sustain them,
Your grace that is all-sufficient
Until they reach their heavenly home.

For there in the Divine glory
They will sing the praise
Of Him who died.
They will drink of the everlasting streams
And dwell in His presence
For evermore.

Not ashamed

Ashamed of You, my God,
I can never be.
Vile sinner though I am,
You made me your son
And gave me a new name
Written on the palms of Your hands,
Stamped on Your forehead indelibly.
I am Yours and will forever be.

Ashamed of You, my Jesus,
I can never be.
You purchased my salvation
By Your blood, shed for me.
You called me Your brother
And brought me into Your family,
Made me Your own.
I am Yours and will forever be.

Ashamed of Your cross
I will never be.
On that wood of shame,
Accursed, You gave Yourself for me.
You bought my redemption
When you bore my sins.
How can I be ashamed
Of You, Christ crucified?

Ashamed of Your suffering people
I will never be.
For they walk the path You trod,
The path of pain and shame.
Falsely accused, reviled, condemned,
Faithful unto death,
They gave their all for you, their Master and King.
How can I be ashamed of them?
Ashamed of Your Gospel, Lord,
I will never be.
Your message of hope
That alone can set us free
From the tyranny of sin,
This eternal message
Of Divine Truth revealed
I will forever proclaim.

Ashamed to be Your servant, Lord,
I will never be.
To sound forth the Gospel message,
To serve You
As You saved me
For You came not be served
But in sacrifice to give.
How can I be ashamed of You?
Ashamed to suffer for Your Name,
I will never be.
To bear your marks on my body
So let it be.
How can I deny Thee, when Thou didst not deny me?
To boast in You is all I seek
And to suffer for Your sake.
How can I be ashamed of Thee?

Will You be ashamed of me, O Lord,
When I stand before Your throne
On the Judgment Day,
My sins laid bare,
My motives and all thoughts made plain?
Faithful I pray I will be,
Ever loyal to the unashamed.

Love

Who are these, my lowly brothers and sisters,
Bereft of love, abandoned, sick, alone?
In prison they dwell, strangers to all.
Sons of Adam? Yes they are, but more!
Children of the second Adam
Bought by Jesus' blood, born of His spirit,
Brothers and sisters now to Him,
Bone of His bone, flesh of His flesh, blood of His blood,
Light of His life, love of His heart, His own beloved.

Hungry was I,
In desperate want,
And you gave Me food,
Food to satisfy.
But when, O Lord?
When did I feed You?
For I see You not
But with the eye of faith.
When with the food you satisfied
The least of My brothers and sisters
Then you saw Me,
Then you served Me.

Thirsty was I,
In desperate need,
And you gave Me water,
Water to refresh.
But when, O Lord?
When did I give You a drink?
For I see You not

But with the eye of faith.
When with water you refreshed
The least of My brothers and sisters
Then you saw Me,
Then you served Me.

A stranger was I,
In desperate want,
And you gave Me a home,
A shelter, a welcome.
But when, O Lord?
When did I give You a home?
For I see You not
But with the eye of faith.
When you invited in
The least of My brothers and sisters
Then you saw Me,
Then you served Me.

Naked was I,
In desperate need,
And you gave Me clothing,
My shame to remove.
But when, O Lord?
When did I dress You?
For I see You not
But with the eye of faith.
When you gave garments to
The least of My brothers and sisters
Then you saw Me,
Then you served Me.

Sick was I,
In desperate pain,
And You cared for me,
Restored me to health.
But when, O Lord?
When did I tend You?
For I see You not
But with the eye of faith.
When you brought healing to
The least of My brothers and sisters
Then you saw Me,
Then you served Me.

Imprisoned was I,
In desperate need,
And you came, and your presence,
Dispelled all My fears.
But when, O Lord?
When did I visit You?
For I see You not
But with the eye of faith.
When you brought comfort and hope to
The least of My brothers and sisters
Then you saw Me,
Then you served Me.

And on that glorious Judgment Day
King Jesus, seated on His throne,
With holy angels hovering round,
Will gather all creation to Him.
And then the King will
Separate
Them,
Separate
That vast unnumbered crowd.
Into His Kingdom, He will bring
Those who cared for Him
By caring for the least and lowliest
Of His brothers and His sisters.

They will feast on heavenly manna,
They will drink from healing streams,
Embraced by everlasting arms.
Clothed in celestial garments fair,
Free from sickness, free from pain
Free from all suffering.

But what of those
Who cared not for the least of His brethren,
Who rejected their Brother and King?
Eternal, everlasting
Separation
From
God

Lift up holy hands

Prayers for the persecuted Church

*"He has delivered us from such a deadly peril, and he will deliver us
again. On him we have set our hope that he will continue to deliver us, as
you help us by your prayers. Then many will give thanks on our behalf for
the gracious favour granted us in answer to the prayers of many."*

—2 Corinthians 1:10-11

The Lord's Prayer in time of persecution

Our Father in heaven,
Abounding in love and mercy,
In our sorrows and joys,
Whom we worship alone,
Holy is Your Name
And honoured in our lives.
In our suffering or dying be honoured.
Your Kingdom come
In this world of sorrow and pain.
Let Your will be done
In heaven and earth
Through your persecuted Church.
Feed us with Your heavenly manna
That we may hunger no more.
In our sinfulness, let Your mercy and forgiveness abound.
Through the fiery heat of temptation
Let Your guiding hand lead us in right paths
That we may not deny Your Name, or bring You shame.
Deliver us from the schemes of the evil one
Who seeks to destroy Your beloved people.
Keep our eyes on Your glorious Kingdom,
As we wait expectantly for Your glorious reign in power
As our eternal King.

Amen

God of all compassion

God of all compassion,
Visit your suffering people.
In the time of their troubles,
Let them not be dismayed.
In their oppression,
Let them not be destroyed.
In their anxiety,
Let them not lose hope.
In their alienation and wandering,
Be their identity and home.

O God, the Father of all mercies,
Look upon them with Your favour.
Set Your seal upon their foreheads.
Let Your right hand uphold them,
Your love encourage them,
Your presence engulf them,
Your protection cover them.
In their fragility and brokenness
Be their strength and treasure.
Let your light shine upon them
And reveal the glory
Of Your eternal Son,
In Whose Name we pray.

Amen

Lord Jesus, Your family are hungry

Lord Jesus,
Your family are hungry,
They are in want of food.
Father, feed them
All: **From Your gracious loving hand.**

Lord Jesus,
Your family are thirsty,
They are in want of refreshment.
Father, give them water
All: **In Your abundant mercy.**

Lord Jesus,
Your family are strangers,
They are in want of acceptance,
Father, give the a home
All: **According to Your lovingkindness.**

Lord Jesus,
Your family are naked,
They are in want of covering.
Father, give them clothes
All: **According to the riches of Your grace.**

Lord Jesus,
Your family are sick,
They are in want of care.
Father, heal them
All: **In Your unfailing compassion.**

Lord Jesus,
Your family are in prison,
They are in want of hope.
Father, sustain them
All: **With Your everlasting faithfulness.**

Gracious and eternal God of love,
Hear our prayer,
In the Name of Your Son Jesus Christ.

Amen

God of grace

God of grace,
Look upon Your suffering people.
In their distress, hear their cry.
Save them from those that seek to harm them.
From violence deliver them
And grant them protection from their enemies.

God of goodness,
Look upon Your wandering people.
In their alienation, hear their cry.
Homeless, vulnerable refugees and sojourners,
From rootlessness deliver them
And grant them a resting place here on earth.

God of mercy,
Look upon Your hungry people.
In their need, hear their cry.
Famished, thirsty, sick, exhausted,
From poverty and destitution deliver them
And grant them provision from Your bounty.

God of justice,
Look upon Your hurting people.
In their shame, hear their cry.
Save them from injustice and false accusation.
From cruel lies deliver them
And grant them vindication.

For You, O Lord Jesus, were reviled,
You were abused and falsely accused.

You were dependent for Your daily bread.
You, a refugee and wanderer,
Had nowhere to lay Your head.
You fell into the hands of violent men.

So feed Your people with the manna from above.
Give them to drink from Your life-giving streams.
Deliver them from all evil
And guide them to their heavenly Home.

In Your Name we pray,

Amen

O triune God

O Triune God, Maker and Creator of all that exists, bringer
of salvation and the hope of Your people, we come before
You to pray for our suffering brothers and sisters who this day
experience discrimination, marginalisation, alienation, injustice,
hatred and persecution, just as Jesus Himself suffered on earth.

Father of Your suffering people, we **adore** You and bless You for
Your power, greatness and covenant love. We **confess** that we
have neither remembered nor cared for Your suffering children.
We **thank** You that Your Name is written on their foreheads,
that they are held in the palm of Your hand, and carried in Your
arms. We **supplicate** You to bring them aid, and gather them
to Yourself when their time on earth is over, and we pray for
ourselves that You would give to us true compassion for them.

Son of our loving Father God, Brother and Kinsman of Your
suffering people, we recognise that Your Body is again being
broken, as Your people suffer at the hands of their tormentors.
Fill them with Your love and forgiveness, as You extended Your
love and forgiveness on the cross to those who persecuted You.

Holy Spirit, the Strengthener of Your suffering people, give
them your grace to sustain them in their trials, Your counsel to
provide wisdom to know how to respond, and Your perseverance
to enable them to endure faithfully to the end.

O Triune God, we pray for the persecutors of Your people that they will experience Your compelling love that casts out all fear and hatred, and will turn their hearts to You.

We pray these things in the Name of the Father, the Son and the Holy Spirit.

Amen

Bring hope, O Lord

Bring hope, O Lord,
To Thy suffering people.
In their anguish and pain,
Be Thou their hope.

Bring hope, O Lord,
To Thy persecuted people.
In their despair,
Be Thou their hope.

Bring hope, O Lord,
To Thy needy people.
In their hunger and thirst,
Be Thou their hope.

Bring hope, O Lord,
To Thy dying people.
In the hour of their death,
Be Thou their hope.

In the Name of Jesus our hope,

Amen

A prayer for the suffering Church

Almighty and most loving God,
the Father of all mercies and God of all consolation,
whose compassion never fails,
save Your persecuted people.

As they pass through the waters of adversity,
may the rivers not overwhelm them.
As they walk through the fires of affliction,
may the flames not consume them.

Give them:
> Your aid, for they are needy,
> Your strength, for they are helpless,
> Your hope, for they are in despair,
> Your deliverance, for they are in danger.

O God,
> make them firm in their faith
> make them joyful through hope,
> fill them with Your love,
> protect them from the wiles of the devil
>> and the conspiracies of men

So that, passing through the waters,
they may come at last to the land of everlasting life,
there to reign with You forever.

In the Name of the all-powerful and triune God, Father, Son
and Holy Spirit,

Amen

O Lord, deliver them

Come, O Lord, and save Your suffering people.
In their distress and anguish, rescue them.
Bring them aid and deliverance by Your power.
Turn Your eyes upon them,
Enfold them in Your arms,
Keep them close to Your heart,
And sustain them by Your presence.

From Satan's hand, keep them.
From Satan's conspiracies, save them.
From Satan's destructive powers, deliver them.
From Satan's slanderous accusations, guard them.
From Satan's lies and deceit, enlighten them.

O Lord, deliver them from the evil one.
Given them faith to stand against the works of Satan,
Protect them with the blood of the Lamb,
Make them faithful in the word of their testimony,
Give them grace to embrace a martyr's death.
Embolden them with courage,
And grant them victory over the power of evil.

In Christ's Name we pray,

Amen

Triumphant martyrs

"'They triumphed over him
by the blood of the Lamb
and by the word of their testimony;
they did not love their lives so much
as to shrink from death."

—Revelation 12:11

Of whom the world was not worthy

Like Him
They have nowhere to lay their head.
Like Him
They have need of food and drink.
Like Him
They wander reviled and despised.
Like Him
They are falsely accused.
Like Him
They suffer ignominy and shame.
Like Him
They are imprisoned and condemned.
Like Him
They die.

Like Him
They will be vindicated.
Like Him
They will rise triumphant.

Your people

O Lord, in You we put our trust
For our bodies are mere vessels of clay,
Weak, fragile, vulnerable, easily broken.
Sustain Your people by Your Divine power
That the radiance of Your life and light may shine on them.

O Lord, in You I put my trust
For evil abounds and traps are set for me.
False accusers rise up
And spread malicious lies and falsehood.
O good Lord, deliver me.

O Lord, let not Your people be crushed.
Grant them the peace beyond understanding.
Lift them out of the depths of despair
And give them Hope.
Lift them up from where they lie trampled
And give them Your Divine strength to go on.
In their afflictions, comfort them.
In their trials, strengthen them.
When their strength is gone, grant them Your strength.

For You are their home
In whom they dwell.
For You are their life
In whom they live.
For You are the air which they breathe.
With You they are accepted, beloved.
For you are the Son,
In this they have their being.

O Lord, Your people are bruised and broken,
Their lands ravaged,
Their homes destroyed,
Their churches deserted,
Their children distraught.

O Lord, Your people are fleeing
With nowhere to go.
Unwanted, they roam,
Seeking a homeland,
A place of safety.
Refugees and exiles in a foreign land,
Aliens who do not belong.
They weep and mourn
As they remember lives past
And joys spent.

Living martyrs they are
For in their faithfulness to You
They suffer loss and privation,
Pain and even death.
Their testimony remains pure
For they count not their lives or loss
For the sake of following You.

You, O Lord, will vindicate,
You will lead them in triumph,
You will embrace them in Your everlasting arms
When You welcome them into heaven's home at last.

The pit is dug

The pit is dug
The trap is laid
The net made ready.
Behind each bush
The stalking enemy hides
To seek my destruction.
So he waits
That fateful day
That will be my end.

Abide, O my soul,
In the Divine Love
That alone can allow
The soul to sing,
The heart to rejoice.
For there is nothing lacking
For God is with me
And I will not be dismayed.

O Lord, do not forsake Your people
In the hour of their trial.

The triumphant martyrs

Lift the standard high
With the emblem of the cross.
Call the soldiers of Christ to battle
For war has been declared
Betwixt Christ and Satan.

Fierce is the battle in the heavenlies.
It reaches down to earth with deadly force
For there Satan pursues the people of God
With grim determination to deceive, to destroy
So they are no more.

But triumph reigns and salvation comes.
Victory is proclaimed for Christ the battle won.
With the saints in His victory train.
They march triumphant
Onward into glory.

There the blood-stained garments are presented
For faithful they have been unto death,
They denied not their Lord,
Having loved not their lives,
They bore witness to Him.

In glorious array in heaven they throng
With songs of everlasting joy
They sing of Him who loved them and gave
That they may know life
And suffer no more.

He is their glory and their head,
Their glory and crown.
He their delight and life
He the radiance that shines greater
Than sun and moon
And all the stars.

And so around the throne the martyrs sing:
Worthy, O worthy art Thou
O Lord our God.
For to You alone belong the glory, honour and power.
For You are the creator of all
And in You alone they live.

Desiring God

"One thing I ask from the LORD,
this only do I seek:
that I may dwell in the house of the LORD
all the days of my life,
to gaze on the beauty of the LORD
and to seek him in his temple."

— Psalm 27:4

O my Lord

O my Lord
O my Lord
Come to me
Come to me
Who are You?
What are You?
O my Lord
I seek Your presence
I seek Your presence
Do not forsake me
Do not forsake me
O my Lord
O my Lord
I cleave to You
I cleave to You
I worship You
I worship You
O my Lord
O my Lord
Do not leave me
Do not leave me
Forsake me not
Forsake me not
O my Lord
O my Lord
Come to Your garden
O my Lord
See the beauty of Your creation
O my Lord
Smell the scent of intoxication

The flowers are radiant
In the precious green grass
O my Lord
The birds sing
To the fountains' music
The trees dance
All glimmer and shine
Iridescent
The sun is bright on the water
Warm is the day
Cool the evening
O my Lord
Delight in Your bounty
O my Lord
I await You
O my Lord
Embrace Your garden
Let her be Your delight
The light is dancing
The fountains play
The waters glimmer
Shadow and night no more
Only perpetual light
There is a river
That flows through the garden
Bringing with it life
Life for evermore
Tree of life
True as a tree
Planted beside the river
A tree of life
Life that never dies

Cause me to drink
O Lord
From Your river of life.
O my Lord
To eat
Fruit from your eternal tree of life

Gazing on my Beloved's face

On my Beloved's face I gaze
And see that marred visage
Those eyes full of tenderness
And wonder.

Gaze I on my Beloved's face
With wonderment,
I see those loving eyes
Set upon me, His beloved.

He who for me has suffered
Such grief and agony
Yet looks upon me
With tenderness and compassion.

I who, though unworthy,
Vile and full of sin,
Am drawn into His loving embrace
By that look of infinite forgiveness and grace.

On my Beloved's face I gaze
To know that rapture of Divine grace
That eludes time and space
And turns the world into a haze.

Lost in those tender eyes
Where nought but peace resides
Where sin and self subside
My soul at last can hide.

My Beloved gazes on me

Gaze I on my Beloved's face
With wonderment
I see those loving eyes
Set upon me, His beloved.

He who for me has suffered
Such grief and agonising pain
Upon me He looks
With eyes of gentleness and tenderness

I unworthy, vile and full of sin,
I am drawn into His loving embrace
And consumed by matchless love,
By infinite forgiveness,
By overwhelming grace

Gazing at each other

On His beloved face I gaze
Wracked by anguish and sorrow,
Yet those eyes full of tenderness
Are fixed on me,

On me who caused the pain
And shared in the cruelty
Yet there is naught but love
For a sinner such as me

What was it that led You there,
My Lord, to that cruel cross of hope
To suffer such agony?
True love, undying love for me.

As you, my Beloved, gaze on me
Your compassion captures my heart
And rapture fills my soul
For You, my precious Lord.

My Beloved's gaze, fall on me
When I my last dying breath will take,
By faith let me clasp Your dying form
As Your loving gaze welcomes me home.

Non Nisi Te, Domine

Gazing on my crucified Lord,
I heard His gentle voice.
'What should I do for you,
You who are my servant?
Is it for you to be famous,
To be lord over many?
Is it to be successful
In all your tasks and service?
Is it to be free from burdens and cares
And to have sufficient and be at ease?
Is it to be protected from all evil and disease
And to have a life free from anguish and pain?

And as I gazed my trembling heart melted
For how could I seek glory
when He was shamed,
Seek to be master of many
when He was servant of all?
How could I seek worldly success
When He died in seeming failure?
How could I seek my wellbeing
When He had nowhere to lay His head?
How could I seek freedom from suffering
When He was crucified for me,
Me a sinner, worthless and vile?

What should I answer?
'Lord, nothing except you -
To gaze into Your face
And to see its radiance,
To behold Your beauty
And be lost in adoration,
To live in Your presence
And desire You alone,
To have the beatific vision
In my flesh, in this my life.
Lord, nothing except you.
Nothing but you, Lord.'

Job 19:26, Psalm 27:4

What is hope?

*"'For I know the plans I have for you,' declares the L*ORD*, 'plans to prosper you and not to harm you, plans to give you hope and a future.'"*

—Jeremiah 29:11

Hope awakening

Death reigns
Life spent
Needlessly
Forlorn I rise
Hope awakening
Purpose
Life begins
New start
Meaning unfolds
Rest

Hope

Hope are You, my Lord,
The bringer of hope,
The purchaser of hope,
Hope for the hopeless
Hope for the suffering
Hope for the lost
Hope for those alone
Hope for the desperate
Hope for the helpless
Hope in life
Hope in death
Eternal and everlasting hope
Are You, my Lord.

Good Lord, protect me

With chains of hope
You bind me.
Wrestle as I might,
I cannot be free.
From Your loving arms
Nothing can separate me.

In darkest night
And deepest gloom
You lead me by Your hand.
You hold me.
In Your everlasting arms
I rest,
Gazing on Your loving face
From which springs eternal hope.

Through the terrors of the night
You lead me,
And from the heat of the noon day sun
You cover me.
From the enemies that surround me
You protect me.
From traps and baseless malicious accusations
You defend me.
For You are supremely good.
For You are my defence,
My just Judge.

Good Lord,
Lead me.
Good Lord,
Cover me.
Good Lord,
Protect me.
Good Lord,
Defend me.

Without Him we can do nothing

Him we worship and praise.
Him we acknowledge
Without Him we can do nothing.
With Him we can do all things.

Deep in my heart

Deep in my heart
My soul yearns for hope.
Through the pain and suffering
I look back to Calvary's Tree
And see Him who died for me.
I see the scarlet thread
That binds me to Him,
That binds Him to me.
My hope will not be lost.

Hope that bridges pain
That bears the anguish and the grief
That holds me fast
Bound by invisible silken threads
Knotted, that cannot be broken,
Making me a Reason to Hope.
My hope will not be lost.

Flee then to despair I cannot
For bound I am
Submission and new eyes
To see the coming dawn
To dawn with the rising Son
Risen for me, my eternal Hope.
My hope will not be lost.

Yea, my soul yearns for hope
To see a glimmer of light
In deepest darkness
To hear a soothing voice
And know that all is well
In the tumults of life
To know that all is well.
My soul, hope thou in God,
God who alone in They salvation
My hope will not be lost.

Deep in my heart
My soul yearns for rest
Turning to Christ,
My eternal Hope.

Bind me with hope to set me free

O hope that binds me to Thee
With cords of love
That cannot be broken.
With cord so fine, with silken threads,
Weave all of my life's suffering and pain.

Thy hope, O Lord, binds Thee to me
With cords that cannot be broken
Its silken threads scarlet be.
Weave them together to set me free
To serve Thee in perfect liberty.

What is hope?

I do not fear
Whatever befalls
For I am carried
In the palm of Your hand.
A friend I am
Of One who never forsakes,
Who will bear me in His arms
Through all life's fiery trials.

Limitless love

"Many waters cannot quench love;
rivers cannot sweep it away."

—*Song of Songs 8:7*

What love is this?

What love is this,
As strong as death, that cannot end,
And reaches limitless, across the universe,
Embracing all, and even me?
A love Divine, a matchless love,
The deep, deep love of Jesus.

What love is this
That triumphs in the face of death
Unconquered, undefeated?
Through agony of soul and body,
Emptied of anger or bitterness,
This love overflows.

What love is this,
Welcoming the kiss
Of friend turned foe,
Embracing the traitor
In his act of treachery?
Love of the betrayed for the betrayer.

What love is this
That serves the selfish
In their wondering pride?
Stripped of all, with towel and basin,
Love stoops to wash,
And then to give His life.

What love is this
That the Creator of the universe,
Emptied of His power and glory
Comes amongst the earthly proud,
The vain, ambitious, status-seekers,
As One who serves?
What love is this

That, though disowned, denied,
By those who claimed to love Him back,
Loves still with endless love?
Loves fully though forsaken?
This is the love that never fails.

What love is this
That loves the bragging coward,
Unlovely and unlovable,
So soon to flee?
This is the love unquenched by many waters,
The love that never ends.

What love is this
That conquers all,
A love commanded, love supreme?
Beloved Jesus, teach us, fill us,
So all may see
That we are Yours, O King of love.

Song of Songs 8:6

He brought love where there was hate

He the Lord of heaven and earth,
Sovereign majestic King of the universe,
Ruler and Sustainer of all life,
All for love's sake
Descends to earth and becomes man.
Taking human flesh, He enters into humanity,
Divests Himself of all riches and honour,
He becomes a Servant
And so the Lord of Glory
Becomes man's Slave.
The Divine incarnate,
In poverty He lives,
With nought but the clothes on His back,
Devoid of all things, destitute He lives,
Dependent, yet serving,
With never-ending compassion,
The weak, the vulnerable, the rejected, the infirm.
Whilst poor, yet making others prosper,
Out of His bountiful mercy and grace,
He brought love where there was hate.

Love, life, light

Love of my love
The love that knows no end
Captivating the heart
Possessing the soul
Unlimited and unbounded
Unmeasured in all its fullness
For me a sinner who was slain
And love, endless love
Conquers
And so, defeated,
I embrace that all-conquering love
And love that love that lovest me.

Life of my life
Life that knows no end
Undefeated in death
Flows like a river
Ever moving
Onward, forward, upward
To Thy glorious rest above.

Light, what radiant bright
Illuminates the darkness
Driving away the shadows

Love of my life
Light of life
Life of my life
With love's fullness
Life possesses
With light undimmed
Life radiates
With life, eternal life.

Love of my life
Light of my love
With love I love Thee, who lovest me
And gave light to my life,
Who enlightens my darkness,
With light I gaze upon Him
The light of lights,
With life the Creator of all life,
I give Him back the live I owe
And love Him with
The love He lovest me.

Limitless love

Love awakens love
That finds its fulfilment
In deepest love
That flows from eternal springs.
Such love is limitless
Having no end.
Absolute is the
Totality of that love.
Endless are its dimensions
Having neither length nor breadth
Nor height not depth
Is that love of Christ
In all its fullness
Vast as the universe
Unmeasured its scope
Rolling as a mighty ocean
In its fullness over me.
Reaching into the very depths of being
Love binds me to Thee
Love embraces
A soul possessed
And a soul possesses
The fire of love.

I awake with You

"When I awake, I shall be satisfied with seeing your likeness."

—Psalm 17:15

The death of death

Death comes, and grief follows in its train.
Unconsolable sorrow breaks the heart,
Life is emptied of purpose
For the tears of love are spent
Leaving but an aching void.
The beloved is no more.
Death knows no end, for it
Is the second certainty.
As with life, so there is death.

Yet death must die
For life to live
The death of death by the death of death
Must see death slain.

As the first Adam died
So too the Second Adam
And with His death defeated death.
Now death has lost its sting,
The grave its victory.

Death is but the gateway to life;
It heralds the dawn
And ushers in the day.
The night of darkness is banished,
Light shines transcendent
With rays of eternal hope.
Sorrow's gone, grief assuaged,
The void is filled, love restored.
Heavenly bliss possesses the soul
And death is no more
For life and love live in God.

O noble death

O noble death
Thee I embrace
With willingness
I give myself to thee.
For what meaning is life
If it knows naught but shame
If it has no dignity or worth
For honour I sacrifice
That death may announce
My victory and triumph

To awake comforted

Death
Blessed release
From all of
Life's sorrows.
To awake
Comforted
In the eternal arms
Where pain
Is no more
And only
Everlasting
Bliss
Awaits the blessed.

Meditation on Psalm 23

The Lord my Shepherd is
In times of want
He provides for my every need.
In times of distress
He gives me rest.
In times of turmoil
He restores my soul.
In the waters
I find refreshment.
In the green pastures
I am sustained.
In the valley of shadows,
Where death lurks,
He takes away the fear.

With His rod He guides me,
As with His staff He protects,
Into His banqueting house
Where He feeds me
Till life's days are done.
The Lord my Shepherd continues to be.

My eternal Friend

Jesus is my eternal companion
In Your birth my fragility You took
In Your life my vulnerability You shared
In Your death my sins You washed away
In resurrection a new life You gave me
In heaven for me You pray
In my death You welcome me
Jesus my Friend
    in life, in death, in eternity

A prayer in the hour of death

In this hour of my death
I entrust myself into Your loving care.
Release me, O Lord,
From all fear and anxiety.
Give me that confidence
To embrace You, my Lord.
Give me that faith to see
The heavenly kingdom that awaits me.
To You I commit now my soul.
Forgive me my many sins and failures
By Your great mercy.
Take my hand,
O my beloved Lord,
And lead me Home
So that when I awake
I awake with You.

Amen

Index
of titles and first lines

For more information on the persecuted Church
please visit
barnabasfund.org